Counting Reindeer

Counting Book For Toddlers
Coloring Book Included

Brenda J. Sullivan
Kathryn A. Sullivan

Counting Reindeer

ISBN: 978-1-7329990-4-6

Published by Tree Roots Press

Photography
Brenda J. Sullivan
Artwork
Brenda J. Sullivan
Kathryn A. Sullivan
Google Creative Commons Images
Pixabay
Canva
Edited by Paul F. Sullivan

Requests to publish work from this book should be sent to:
Treerootspress@gmail.com
brenda@brendajsullivanbooks.com

Tree Roots Press

treerootspress.com

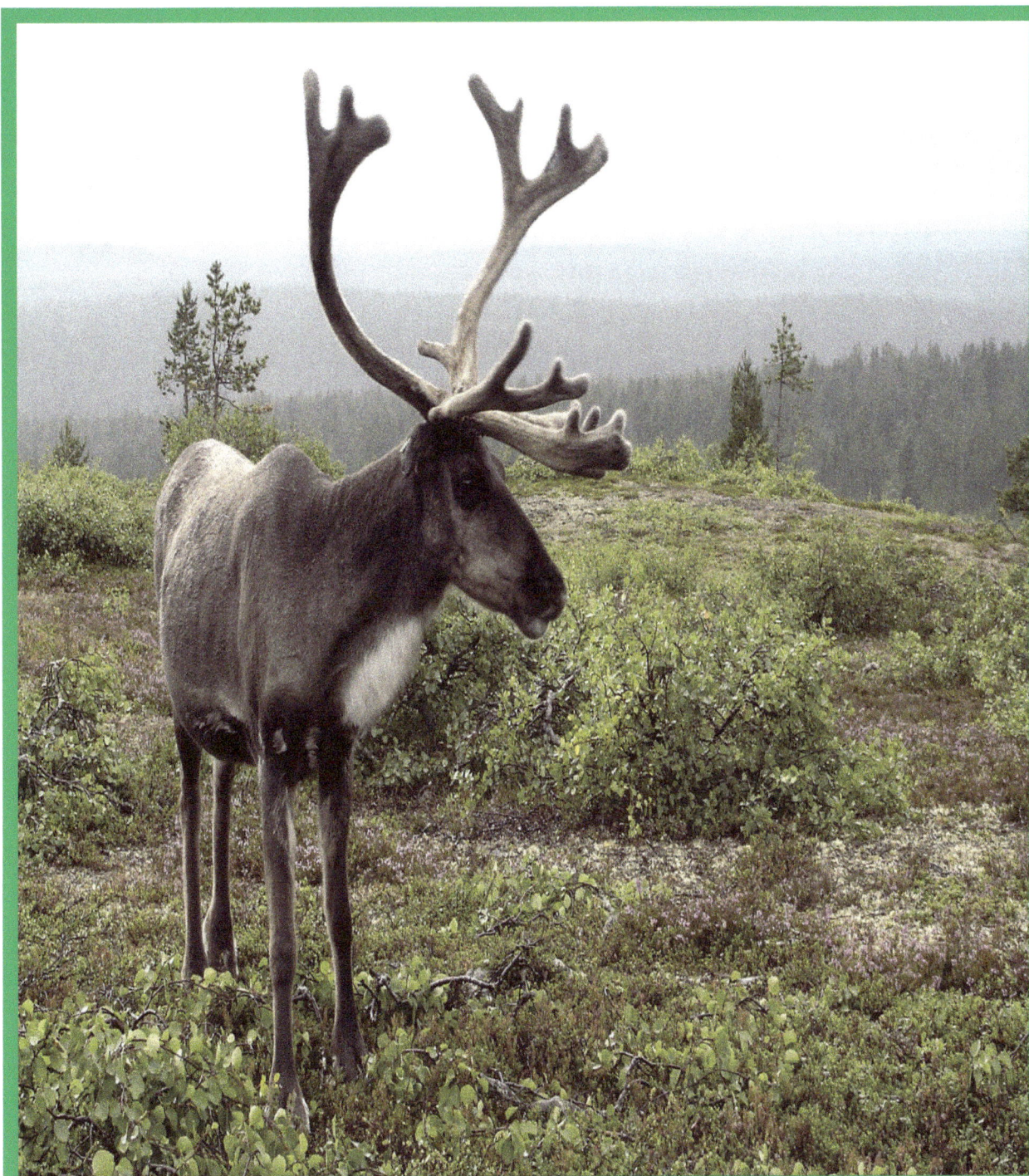

This book is dedicated to Katie's doctors, her homecare nurse, Gail and the medical support staff at Connecticut Children's Medical Center.
Words cannot express how grateful we are for all your support over the years.
Thank you!

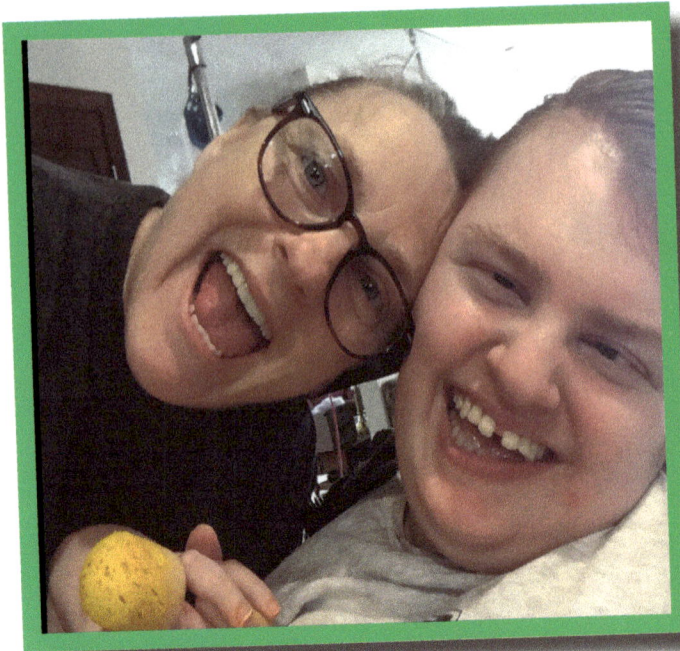
Katie with Mommy being silly while we paint

Katie with Daddy on one of our beach walks

Katie finishing up one of her whale pictures. Yes, we paint outside the lines!

Meet the Artist!

Katie is a wheelchair-bound young lady with severe cerebral palsy and epilepsy among many other medical problems. She is also nonverbal with very limited vision. Despite these challenges, she has a fighting spirit and has learned how to use basic communication skills and assistive technology to produce various arts and crafts products.

This is one of Katie's "Able Gifts" – a product she helped create with her Mother, Brenda J. Sullivan, when she is in good health and "able" to do so.

Proceeds are used to support the costs of Katie's craft-works and enable her to more fully engage her world.

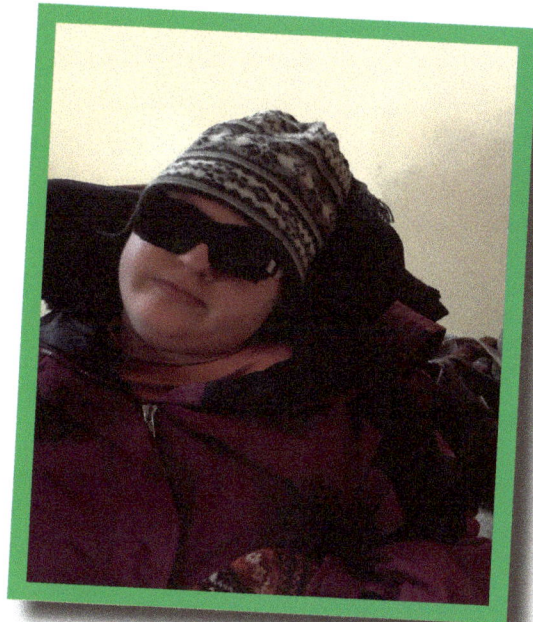

Katie is ready for the snow!

Katie on Christmas Day 2012

1

One Reindeer

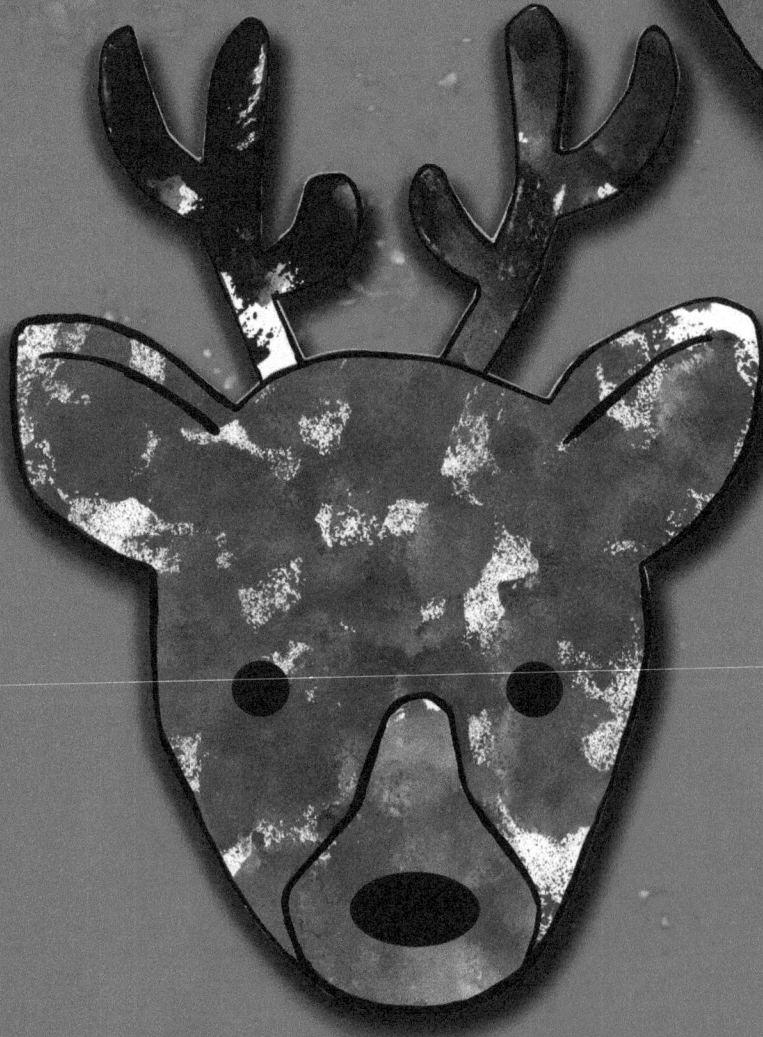

2

Two Reindeer

3

Three Reindeer

4

Four Reindeer

5

Five Reindeer

6

Six Reindeer

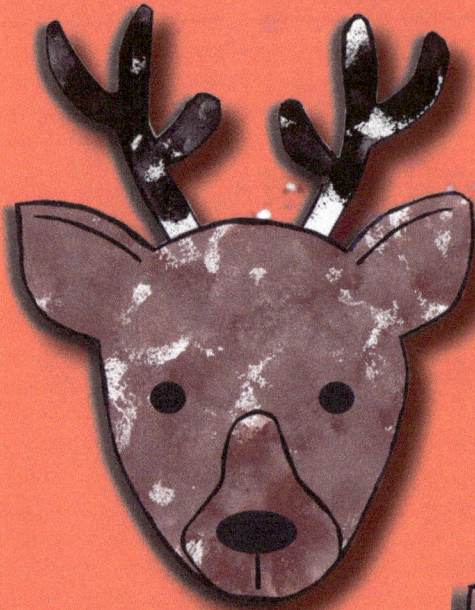

7

Seven Reindeer

8

Eight Reindeer

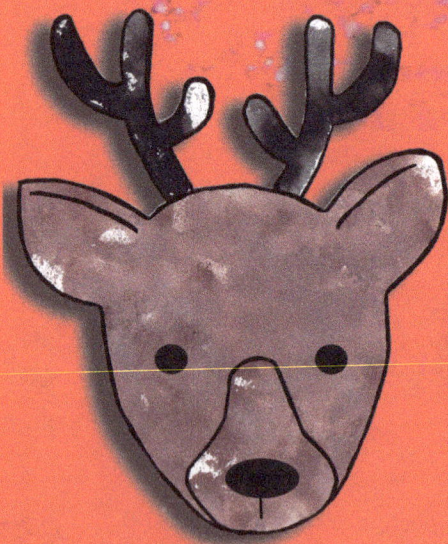

9

Nine Reindeer

10

Ten Reindeer

Reindeer fur is brown and white but there are also rare white reindeer, which have special genes that give them their white color.

To see one of these white reindeer is something very special!

People living in the Arctic depend on reindeer for food, clothing, and shelter. Some Arctic peoples have tamed wild reindeer and take care of them like a herd of cows or sheep.

A reindeer herder can milk a reindeer like a cow for their children to drink.

Reindeer are very social creatures. They feed, travel, and rest in groups called herds, which can range from ten to hundreds of animals.

In the spring, reindeer herds can get even bigger - sometimes between 50,000 to 500,000 members!

How many white reindeer do you see in the picture?

Reindeer are herbivores, which means they only eat vegetation. In one day, they can eat 9 to 18 lbs. of vegetation including herbs, ferns mosses, grasses, shoots, fungi, mushrooms and leaves.

During the winter, reindeer travel between 1000 miles (1,600 km) - 3000 miles (5000 km) looking for food.

This reindeer wants a carrot! Do you have one?

Reindeer are members of the deer species and both females and males grow antlers. This is unusual as only males grow antlers in other related species like white tailed deer and elk. Reindeer antlers are the biggest and heaviest in the deer family.

Fun Facts About Reindeer

These large beautiful creatures are called reindeer in Europe but in the United States and Canada, they are referred to as caribou.

Reindeer are native to the coldest regions of the world - the Arctic, sub-Arctic, tundra, and boreal areas of northern Europe, Siberia, and North America.

In the Nordic lands of Sweden and Finland and in other arctic villages, herders train reindeer to pull a pulk - a special Nordic sled similar to what Santa uses on Christmas Eve.

Many Arctic people believe that a reindeer is a spirit animal symbolizing resourcefulness, wisdom, cleverness, knowledge, and creativity. These animals are honored for their nobility and represent the continuation of the tribe.

1

One Reindeer

2

Two Reindeer

3

Three Reindeer

4

Four Reindeer

5

Five Reindeer

6

Six Reindeer

7

Seven Reindeer

8

Eight Reindeer

9

Nine Reindeer

10

Ten Reindeer

About Our Family

Brenda Sullivan lives in South Glastonbury, CT, with her husband Paul and their daughter Katie.

They are avid nature lovers and gardeners who took their love of gardening to a new level by converting their 1.3 acres into a small farm called Thompson Street Farm LLC.

Brenda is an herbalist and market gardener who specializes in growing lavender, medicinal herbs, and flowers. She also makes handcrafted goat's milk herbal soaps and herbal bath products using the herbs, flowers, fruits, and vegetables grown on their farm or purchased from other local farmers.

Katie, the love of their life and the center of their universe has several serious medical conditions, including severe cerebral palsy, epilepsy, and minimal vision. She is nonverbal and wheelchair-bound, but these challenges have not prevented Katie from experiencing life.

Katie experiences the world on her terms with assistive technology, other sensory adaptations, and years of homeschooling experience. Katie understands basic concepts and has developed many interests, including a music appreciation, painting with her Mother, and listening to stories.

She loves being outdoors, and we've discovered that enabling her to experience the natural world has been Katie's best educator.

Our love of the outdoors has been our inspiration for creating these nature-themed children's books.

Journals

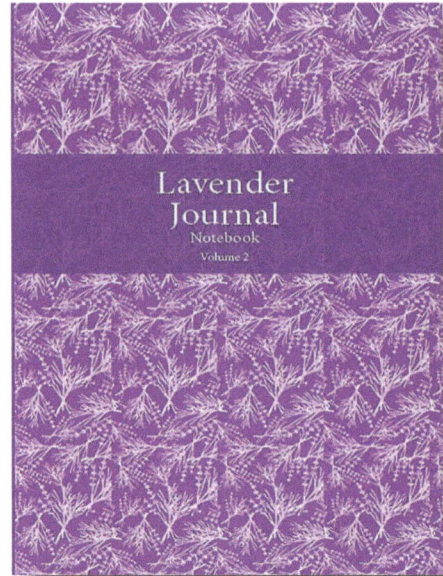

Available on Amazon

Connect with Brenda online:
www.brendajsullivanbooks.com
www.thompsonstreetfarm.com
www.farmtobath.com
www.livingandlovinherbs.com
Facebook.com/brendajsullivanbooks
Facebook.com/livingandlovinherbspodcast

Other Books By Brenda J. Sullivan
Children's Books

Available in all stores and libraries - just ask!

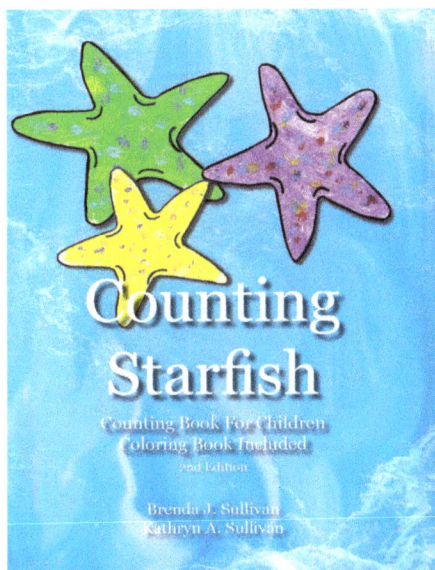

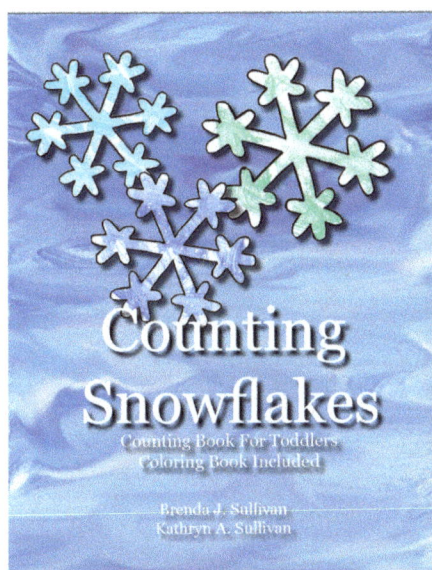

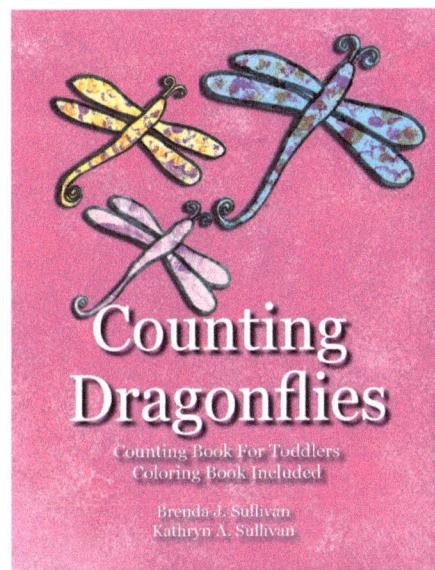

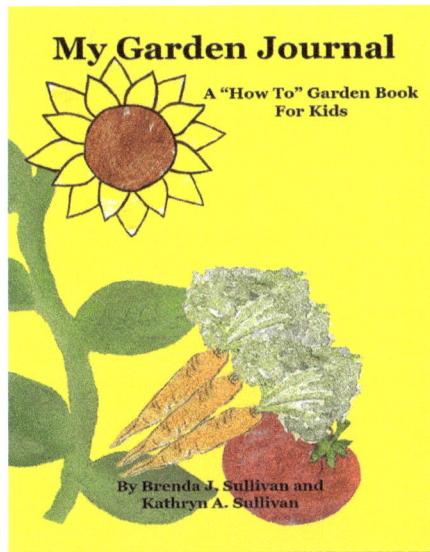

Counting Starfish
Counting Book For Children
Coloring Book Included
2nd Edition
Brenda J. Sullivan
Kathryn A. Sullivan

Counting Snowflakes
Counting Book For Toddlers
Coloring Book Included
Brenda J. Sullivan
Kathryn A. Sullivan

Counting Dragonflies
Counting Book For Toddlers
Coloring Book Included
Brenda J. Sullivan
Kathryn A. Sullivan

My Garden Journal
A "How To" Garden Book For Kids
By Brenda J. Sullivan and Kathryn A. Sullivan

Join our newsletter and learn about our latest book releases and promotions. You will also get progress reports as I work on the newest book project.

www.brendajsullivanbooks.com

www.ingramcontent.com/pod-product-compliance
Lightning Source LLC
Chambersburg PA
CBHW042354030426
42336CB00029B/3482